for *[illegible handwriting]*

hoping you'll ... something
to enjoy among these,

READING A RIVER

Simon

Plymouth Sept '12

READING A RIVER

New & Selected Poems

SIMON CURTIS

Shoestring Press

Typeset and printed by Q3 Print Project Management Ltd, Loughborough, Leics
(01509) 213456

Published by Shoestring Press
19 Devonshire Avenue, Beeston, Nottingham, NG9 1BS
(0115) 925 1827
www.shoestringpress.co.uk

First published 2005
© Copyright: Simon Curtis
The moral right of the author has been asserted.
ISBN: 1 904886 26 4

Shoestring Press gratefully acknowledges financial assistance from Arts Council England

CONTENTS

Acknowledgements

Grateful acknowledgements to the following magazines and newspapers, where many of the poems first appeared: *Acumen, The Australian, The Charles Lamb Society Bulletin, Critical Quarterly, Critical Survey, The Dark Horse, Encounter, The Independent, The Interpreter's House, London Magazine, London Review of Books, New Welsh Review, Poetry Durham, Quadrant* (Australia), *The Spectator, The Times Literary Supplement, Verse.*

Most of the poems were published in the following collections: *On the Abthorpe Road* (Davis Poynter, 1975), *Mrs Payne* (NW Arts chapbook, 1979), *Faber Introduction 6* (1985), *Sports Extra* (Littlewood, 1988), *Views* Northamptonshire Poems with wood-engravings by Ian Stephens RE (Northampton, 1990), *The Chronometer* (Paperback Press, Sydney chapbook, 1990), *Twenty Sonnets and a Coda* (Poet and Printer chapbook, 1993) and *Spike Island Spring* (Shoestring Press chapbook, 1996).

In loving memory

DHC
VMSC
JJMC

BOUNDARY LANE

Where Boundary Lane skirts high-rise Hulme,
What looks at first a fly-tip site –
Old bricks, ground elder and drab grass –
Has bluebells, too; its yeast of bloom.
One consequence of planning blight.

And in its inner city lung
Behind the Dar-ul-Amaan Club
And Lee's Kebab and Chicken place
Some goldfinches are scavenging
For thistle-seed among the scrub.

For all its wear, its traffic-fumes,
This frayed and dingy habitat
Deserves its due, distinctive gloss:
A *charm* of goldfinches. And Hulme's.
An offchance worth no less than that.

WHY CLIMB A MOUNTAIN?

Increasingly skew-whiff with each returning year,
the apple-tree boughs grope upwards, grow and sprout
southwards and eastwards out
in order to evade
to north and west the Goliath of a lime's
thick life-denying shade.

Crabwise, inch by inch, the Bramley climbs
its invisible cliff-face crag of light and air.
My tree, slow mountaineer,
goes on, because it's there.

READING A RIVER

A heron lifts away as we approach
Where cloud-grey Hodder and grey Ribble meet;
A spit of stones, an eddy-knuckled reach,
And glassy patch downstream as dark as peat.

There's movement in that pool, see? and you're sure
It's grayling, moving gently to large duns;
The Hodder, there, is acid, from the moor;
That's why it's good for autumn sea-trout runs.

What strikes my eye as surface, April-cool,
You read like braille, uncannily and clear,
Connecting signs of life in flow or pool;
A river's script, and palaeographer.

All waters have their temper, temperament,
Each river-face, its moods and tics and traits,
As individual as a finger-print;
The shoals and shallows, lies below still glaze,

And alders, stoneflies, sedges, each month's hatch
On Coquet, Lathkill, Driffield Beck or Dee;
A living web, I'd say, where you're in touch ...
It's practice, pal, not flaming ESP;

It's try and try, a knack you pick up, right?
And 'knack' for 'art', you speak the northern way,
To deprecate what works like second sight,
Transforming all I saw that cloud-dulled day.

TURK'S HEAD

A beer-gut, bald, and fifty if a day,
He piped old airs, their lilt as good as new,
The Crooked Bawbee first, then *Rothbury Hills*;
Our ring of listeners gathered round and grew –

That pick-up band about him handing on
The tunes across the years, each jig, each dance,
Music that fathers and forefathers played
To young and old as now, no difference.

A lath-lean fiddler, long-nosed girl on flute,
Like faces from a print: *The Fete, Kermesse.*
You joined or left as freely as you liked.
This fete is all fetes in its timelessness:

A noon-time damp-charged sky, a small pub yard,
And *The Carrick Hornpipe* then *Sweet Hesleyside.*

WISH YOU WERE HERE

I tramped alone past limestone chine and bluff,
Up from the wind-vexed sea loch and *machair*.
Heather browned far moorland, curlews cried above,
In trackless leagues I longed that you could share.

With rod and bag I reached the white hotel –
My annexe room, its fifties' furniture;
But missing you, as dark on Fashven fell,
I went to join the anglers in the bar.

The Tweed, the Torridge; grilse and gillaroo;
Tackle, sea-trout, char; days in rain and sun ...
I missed you, yes; with whisky, though, wit grew,
As night-cap followed night-cap, one by one.

So ache of absence eased and, truth to tell,
I sloped off happy, love, to bed; slept well.

JOHN GLOVER

You'd rich success; were called the "English Claude";
Whatever, then, John Glover, made you sail,
An emigrant to far Van Dieman's land –
The Southern Cross above *its* Patterdale?

You'd wealth and, yes, a somewhat laughed-at fame,
An expert at Sublime and Picturesque;
But sold your seat up in the English Lakes
To settle near that quite unenglish Esk.

Did you with sure self-knowledge understand
Your life's work was small beer (each hackneyed view),
But in your bones could also sense you might,
At sixty-three, make up some sort of hand
From Bush and gum and glaring southern light –
Grandfather eyes turned young again, and true?

LCM OR HCF?

Dusty bay at a B-road's edge;
A gate-gap in what's left of hedge.
As I pull in for sun, pipe, view,
A wren lets rip with wrensong, too.

Though quite banal as moment-yield,
Both bird and rough ragworty field
Square perfectly with my *ad hoc*
Middle-of-nowhere dog days stop.

And strange how breaks like this possess
One factor, *sui generis*:
The way dull lay-bys, God knows why,
(Not being Lulworth Cove, Versailles,
Cape Wrath, Dove Cottage or Loch Ness)
Will etch their lines on consciousness.

FITZROY

Calm, like a hands-laid-on, as first light breaks
on the paperbarks' silver-grey frieze,
and a bronzewing flutes his three-note call
across the still creek and trees.

Then a tent-peg clinks, and somebody swears
as they fumble their tent-flap zip;
why shrug, why turn with such chagrin back
to friends, words, fellowship?

IVANHOE, NSW

Unchecked coarse grass, dock and clover
sprout between flags of the swimming-pool steps,
well on their way to greening them over;

there's a bench, upturned, by the pool inside,
while gum-nuts litter dry earth underneath
the deserted playground's swing and slide.

The chanced-upon settlement, sculpture-still,
lies, as if stunned, in the outback glare,
and so eerily silent it seems surreal,

where the only life in the brick-kiln heat –
baking each iron-roofed home in its plot
behind dusty trees in the empty street

as we stretch our limbs and fidget round –
are the irresolute shadow-pools we cast
on the washed-out khaki-coloured ground;

while, scuffed by some wind's breath off the plain,
a sand-plume unfurls in slow motion, like smoke,
to hover, half-billow, then subside again

to the press of heat and the sun-bruised still –
with a sort of shrug at its own lack of will.

LLANDUDNO SEASCAPE, WITH FIGURES

A pewter sea. No fishing smacks or sails.
A seafront palm, dishevelled by March gales.

And framed by wintry skies and low-tide sand,
In overcoats, two grey-haired women stand,

Braving the cold for snapshots on the prom –
One coat Saxe-blue, and one geranium.

Blue holds her brolly up (my, how it blows!)
With arm outstretched, mock Mary Poppins pose,

Then (look you) does a skittish schoolgirl skip
Of unexpected sprightliness, and *click*,

The moment's caught, plus pier and Orme and sea,
Dim Parcio and all. They laugh. Now tea.

Burlesque hit off with unselfconscious ease –
Two sisters – spinsters – lovers – divorcées? –

Without whom I should never have believed
How empty seascapes are when unrelieved.

Dim Parcio, No parking, in Welsh.

IN DUNHAM MASSEY PARK

In black leather jacket and pale blue jeans,
    On her own, unconcerned, in half-sun,
She was walking the broad grassed deer-park ride –
    As a man on his own might have done.

I'd like it, in fact, in Britain today,
    To be perfectly usual to see
What's not so usual – a woman, alone,
    Out walking as she was, and free,

Since that's what she'd simply chosen to do,
    Whether light-hearted or out of sorts,
For the fun or relief of it, solo,
    With her shadow, her dog or her thoughts.

It's not I've some project or programme
    Or social science theory to voice;
Just a yen or a wish that, as men have,
    Women had the scope of that choice –

To go for a tramp and be by themselves,
    Among oaks and head bare to the breeze,
Unanxious, unharassed, quite unremarked,
    And equal and really at ease.

11

JOHN SELL COTMAN AT ROKEBY

If faith can move mountains, so then can art –
As in Cotman's two *Views* of Greta Bridge:
The first features sky while the second depicts
A rugged and blue-shadowed fellside ridge.

All art is selection, as Cotman knew well,
At work on each similar, different scene,
With bogus blue hills for harmony's sake
Or counterfeit sky where hills should have been.

Almighty cheek or rank inconsistency
Or just artist's licence? The verdict depends
On *mimesis*, of course; how far can you go
Shunting landscape round as a means to your ends?

What magical weeks, though; Cotman at Rokeby;
What freshness and rightness of touch and of eye;
When 'ficle Dame Nature' was changed and improved
(Her sky turned to fellside, fellside to sky),

Was it faith of a kind, since a spirit had moved?

KIRKHOUSE

The whinstone sheepfold's been submerged by spruce,
Now they've put Kirkhouse Moor to commercial use;

And in thirty years they'll pick up a return
On their plantation leagues by Paddock Burn,

When the spruce is felled, once fully black and grown –
The sheepfold long since gone to heaps of stone.

Accountants costed what their Board would gross:
The trees their profit – and the moor our loss.

So spruce-rows and gouged ditches, straight as dies,
Stain and deform each hill. It's enterprise.

That change is certain, is a truth as old
As truths the sheepfold stood for, and now sold.

MY TURN

My turn? OK. I throw the dice, get ten,
Glance down to see where boot is on the board,
Then count the squares from Pentonville and land
Slap bang on Vine Street with hotel. Oh *Lord.*

The children burst out laughing, since I'm sunk.
I groan, recount the squares – and play my role,
Knelt round the board with them (and largish scotch),
The grown-up stooge, good loser, life and soul.

I jolly through and trust, Dad, you'd approve
How I, though not as skilled as you were, play –
You gone, your role passed on – and can't but think
Again of you this Borders Hogmanay.
(*A thousand quid? It can't be. Where's my drink ..?*)
The Lord who gave; the Lord who takes away.

GLIMPSE

Below Wylam bridge, alone and absorbed,
An angler casts out. The spring salmon run;
Like new-minted silver, a dazzle downstream,
The Tyne's cold grey glaze transformed by March sun.

Dark shape against shine, in waders he stands,
Where I'd rather be, not car-bound *en route*
For Consett's Dipton crematorium –
In funeral temper, tie and best suit.

No chance, as I pass, of more than a glimpse,
Eyes skinned not for fish but the Whickham signs;
No chance of even the briefest of stops;
Great day, alright; lucky devil; tight lines ...

You lived nearby, and surely would have known
The glimpse, my sense of seize the day and live –
The silvered Tyne, the salmon coming home –
Would understand, lost friend, and would forgive?

PUB LUNCH

"No chips for me", I fussed when you asked,
"I'm keeping an eye on my weight";
Aware, as soon as the words were out,
I'd said the wrong thing, but too late.

You had to build your body-weight up –
So the consultant counselled you;
Though as you couldn't digest solid food,
It wasn't all that easy to do.

Yet in good part, as always of old,
You were quick to relish the joke
(Brother not putting his brain in gear
As per usual before he spoke) –

In the canalside pub at Stoke Bruerne,
As bright, slow narrowboats passed,
And August sun and your birthday, too,
Which we couldn't but know was the last.

WOODBRIDGE

I glimpsed, from the hired limousine,
Two boys, well-scarved against the sleet,

Each with a bright blue sledge, engrossed,
Setting out up the whitened street –

Like you and I, in Lancashire snow,
Long since, not a care in the world.

One hour afterwards, round your grave,
In bitter cold, snow-eddies swirled.

IN MEMORIAM A.M. 1948–1995

As kids traipsed off, in twos and threes,
    To school past pub, past betting-shop,
The sun lit up a crimson blaze
    In kerbside thorn-trees on Moor Top.
My post had brought a hoped-for cheque –
    A friend in France had sent a card –
A day that could have been designed
    To lull and catch one off one's guard.

At nine the phone went, and I heard.
    A heart-attack. At work. You'd died.
I stood there, speechless, while the sun
    Streamed on, mechanically, outside.
Mechanically, it must have lit
    Your Borders valley – Dod Hill Wood,
Lee Pen and white-harled kirk and house;
    Lit shock, lit loss, lit widowhood.

Just two short months ago, I stayed;
    A week when, why, we'd time to spare;
We beat the boys at badminton;
    Heard Brahms quartets down at Traquair;
The inn at Tweedsmuir, where we talked
    Of Health Care Trusts – your work in Fife:
Your team, new colleagues, clinics, plans –
    A twinkle in your eye. New life.

I've snapshots of our long, last hike –
    The heather coming into flower;
Straw-hat and cod Edwardian pose,
    You stand, relaxed, by Blackhouse Tower.
The thistledown on Fethan Hill;
    Curlews above Mountbengerlaw;
The five of us at Tibbie Shiels –
    It seemed such times were all *encore*.

That phone-call morning when I learned
    In brute fact there'd be no again,
The sun streamed through my window-bay;
    A torpid wasp banged at a pane.
"We'll meet at Hogmanay," you wrote
    Three weeks ago, and sent a book
On Scott you'd seen and thought I'd like ...
    Why, there you are by Blackhouse, look.

To try to comprehend, I read
    Donne's famous sermon; *Rasselas*;
Ecclesiastes; *Book of Prayer*;
    Of how man's life is but as grass ...
Yet Sid Scam thrives; Stu Snout-in-Trough;
    Fritz Fraud; Hugh Huckster; and Sam Spiv,
While you, most generous of hosts,
    Had so much yet to do, and give.

To try to comprehend, I write
    Of valley, glebe and burnside trees,
The manse you made (in Hardy's phrase)
    A house of hospitalities –
To build a bridge across the void.
    Words make no sense. What can one say?
We thought we'd time; but we were wrong.
    We will not meet at Hogmanay.

Mechanically, the sun streams down
    On suburb street and shops, the same;
The kids traipse off to school once more;
    The leafless thorns no longer flame.
Mechanically, a curlew calls
    From Dod Hill Wood to Kirkhouse clear;
Hard by glebe-field and Quair, good friend,
    You lie, now, and you cannot hear.

IN MEMORY OF BILL RUDDICK

That time we took the Rydal 'upper path'
  To go to Mattins down in Grasmere church;
    That time on Dodd – wet through from Lakeland rain;
  Tarn Hows, that time, in deep snow one late March –
    I see you gesture, hear your voice again,
      As now the aftermath
Of recollection grows; those good days, gone.
    Faces and scenes from twenty years come back;
    'Viewing' Aira Force; Mirehouse walks; Tarn Beck;
The *George* at Keswick or the Grasmere *Swan* –

Where you'd talk on of Southey, of 'Lodore';
  Of Rugby's Thomas Arnold at Fox How,
    ('Mere mountain and lake hunting is time lost');
  The Wordsworths' early days at Windybrow;
    Dove Cottage, too, and Coleridge as guest –
      I hear your voice once more,
Then see you sat, unwell, two years ago,
    By Bassenthwaite and silhouetted Fells
    You knew and loved – Barf, Causey Pike, Catbells –
The last time we were there; last cameo.

Fleas in the beds at Wythburn when Keats stayed –
  The funny side of things delighted you;
    The 'wretched' Liverpudlian called Crump
Who, building Allan Bank, wrecked Wordsworth's view,
    And put him in the most almighty grump;
      The poem to a spade ...
The flow of anecdotes streams back, pell-mell;
    How Wilkie Collins was laid up, quite lame,
    When he and Dickens (of all people) came;
He'd sprained his ankle up on Carrock Fell.

The jokes went with old-fashioned scholar skills,
  Though "suits", the "men in suits", now call the tune;
    What's "relevant"? What's "new"? But not, what's true? –
  Helm Crag in May, beneath a crescent moon;
    The lovely *Grasmere* Farington once drew,
      Or *Skelwith Force*, by Hills.

Your learning, lightly worn, was shared, no side,
    So willingly with friends; one had a sense
    Of freedom from the grids of relevance.
You were rereading Scott the week you died.

With "suits" now taking over literature,
    The Stokes-Nokes, Hobbs-Nobbs, Boot-Suit Theory type
        All fly their lightweight, opportunist kites,
    As learning's lost in fashion and self-hype;
        Students are "customers"; quotations, "bites" –
            You found the "suits" a bore.
    You'd deprecate the plaudit 'Humanist';
        In truth, Bill, it would well epitomise
        The 'spirit of Elian friendliness'
    You lived for with such humour and such zest.

GLASS

A woman in a parka walks her dogs
On thin grass by the walled-up old wet dock;
From high-rise phosphate plant two men bike home
Along the towpath past pipeline and lock.

A ring of factories hems Spike Island in;
They're there because they're there, and must produce;
Detergents, pharmaceuticals and dyes
Sum fate up, here; fifteen decades of Use.

With haunts more like Giverny or Coole Park
Than grounds like these, leached out by *laissez-faire,*
Creative thoughts move in a higher class?

Yet workmen, woman, dogs; a gathering dark;
Flawed circumstance flawed Everyman must share –
So look, no condescension, in its glass?

TOWARDS FIDDLERS FERRY POWER STATION

A glaze of low-tide mudflats, Widnes marsh,
And in the air a sourish sulphur smell;
Spike Island's trees are saplings, scrub-growth young –
The green of reclamation, you can tell.

United Alkali's old Gossage works
Was flattened to the ground to make this park,
Grass acres ringed by new works' high tech steel,
Pale superstructures floodlit in half-dark.

A word like flange seems coined for such a place;
A chlorine, potash, soap and bleach town, right?
Its Heritage is mass-productiveness.

Beyond the ground which grass and gorse renew,
The huge Rocksavage plant glows, light by light,
With turbines thrumming on, and work to do.

STANLOW

That something as utilitarian
As Stanlow's oil refinery at night
Should glow like distant, silver-pale *grisaille* –
Its fretted steel, a honeycomb of light …

Though functional as prose, there's beauty, too,
In how the floodlit complex strikes the eye;
Reactor vessels; high tech scrubbing towers;
A red flame burning waste off in black sky.

Vaccines to Weedol, bleach to PVC,
Commodities are what such plants produce;
And yet those lights, above the salt-marsh mist,
Create a sort of poetry from Use –
Subverting all we think that Art should be –
Organic in their way, and catalyst.

WIDNES: SPIKE ISLAND SPRING

The old dock mirrors thin all-over cloud –
The sun behind, pale as a watermark;
As blackbirds weave canalside lines of flight,
A couple walk the towpath through the park.

The blackbirds stake their territorial claims
On land with steam-wreathed cooling-towers above;
A line of factories rings the park's lung in,
Where lovers claim their time-off grounds of love

From work and nine-to-five, in weekend ease.
(One plant makes phosphates and another bleach,
Supply. Demand. Free Trade. Commodities).

Past anglers and the bearded boat-club man
They walk the springtime Sunday towpath reach.
You make of where you live the best you can.

SANKEY CANAL

A blackbird flits off low from towpath gorse
Across the silent, algae-choked canal –
So flat and still, it looks like pale green ice.
A tang of acid sours the salt-marsh chill.

As mudflat redshanks pipe thin counterpoint
To winds which fret old signal-box and shed,
All Sunday from the bleak grey phosphate plant
Steel flues spout steam and turbines pulse and thud.

The eye takes in this Widnes winter scene,
And spoil-heaps which rough grass and thorn renew,
The legacies of years of *laissez-faire*;

And then that boat, ablaze with Van Gogh blue –
Its cheerfulness so chronic, it must mean
There's love behind its name, bright *Marie-Claire*.

CHEMICAL

The lung-corroding fumes; back-breaking toil;
The seething spoil-heaps of foul 'galligu';
The sting of chloride acid in the air;
The Mersey killed by toxin residue.

And yet (the 'yet' of Whig progressive views),
For all the cost, there were the benefits:
The medicines; the dyes; the bleach and soap.
The town improved, if once the very pits.

Were Muspratt, Gossage, Castner, Hutchinson,
Hard bastards or far-sighted pioneers?
Or was it mass-production's time had come,
Whose pawns they were as much as profiteers?

Some scars have healed, greened over, anyhow.
Their old wet dock's a lake with herons now.

QUINCE

The quince-tree's in leaf, and shadows the bay-window;
Two blackbirds skitter about
Above the first lilac and windblown red tulips
You say you can just make out.

You can see (more or less) how the ground at the back
Has begun to get overgrown;
But what can you do, with your legs so unsteady,
At ninety, and here on your own?

You peer at the garden, its brightness and shadow,
As springtime renews with a will.
Just the two of us now, who were four, left to hear
The quince-tree bird-song still.

BACK HOME ...

However on earth can I tell you
The snowdrops you planted years since,
In their white and silent dozens,
Are in flower once again by the quince –
To distress you into recalling
The home we insisted you leave?
Is it best, then, not to tell you?
Or is not-to-distress to deceive?

WASPS IN THE HOME

In normal circumstances (which don't pertain),
We would without doubt have taken
The set-back that morning in our stride
Which instead left you very much shaken.

They'd found a wasps' nest up in the eaves,
So indignant wasps were milling about
In the room next to yours. Staff had no choice
But there and then to move you out.

It's like bedlam, you said in your muddle,
And our outing got off to a bad start;
Unforecast rain then compounded ill-luck;
Enough to make anyone lose heart.

We've time though, surely, still, for second thoughts,
To make light of what happened, and agree
What a teacup storm those wasps really were.
Pretend things remain as they used to be.

BREEZY PRESTATYN

Having adjusted the flaps for your feet
   And tucked the rug in round your knees,
I wheel the wheelchair along sand-strewn flags
   On Prestatyn prom in the breeze –
Past a red-head out walking her collie,
   Two youths playing ducks and drakes,
A black-headed gull, clear-etched against blue,
   And breaker's spray-spout as it breaks.

Subjects which Hopkins, who knew this coast well,
   Would without much doubt have imbued,
Thanks to a gift one could call second sight,
   With a sense of infinitude;
Their instress divine and thus radiant,
   An earnest of God-ordained worth –
In contrast to which our presence must seem
   Unradiantly down-to-earth.

If we miss out on the uplift of instress,
   And sell the transcendent short,
This midday hour or so's change of scene
   Is much as we hoped for, and sought;
Where, for all that the prospect is finite,
   You may sit, rug warm round your knees,
Tired eyes drinking in whatever they can
   Of girl, wind-buoyed gull and Welsh seas.

SLOES

Three years ago, I took you in the car
To help with picking sloes to make sloe gin,
By Kingthorn Mill down on the Bradden lane.
It meant a change for you, was not that far,
And you could walk still, then, and so join in.

And now I've come in late September cool,
A hundred miles from Bradden and the mill,
To gather sloes once more, in Manchester,
A rec with traffic noise near Parrs Wood School;
The site has changed, but not the ritual.

Sleeves wringing wet from blackthorn drenched with rain,
I carry back perhaps two pounds of sloes –
Small change of news, as well, to share with you:
"Been busy, Mum! It's sloe gin time again",
Though in the Home you're yonderly, God knows,

In such a state how can you care that much,
For all I'll talk as if we're quite in touch?

WEYMOUTH NIGHTINGALE

As ring-road cars thwacked past the parking spot
Where kissing-gate gives on to reed-beds path,
I picked out, just, his rising, falling song
In air still damp from cloudburst aftermath.

The girl had told me that I'd hear him there,
The nightingale, my May Day singleton,
Secure in fading light and roadside gorse,
His journey out of Africa now done.

Those haunting, half-heard notes were something, too,
That if you could, you would have loved to share,
Asleep now in the Home, ten miles away,
Your brain confounded by dementia;

A song which must, instead, suffice as news
To talk of when I come tomorrow night,
For all I'm doubtful if you'll take it in …
To think of journey's end, though; fading light;

And nightingales that once you told me of,
In Towcester churchyard, forty years ago –
So much floods back to mind, of worth, of loss,
Of time that's gone, and debt of thanks I owe.

COLLEAGUE

Our colleague, Ernest Young, expounds
    To first year 'kids' upon
Metadiegetic discourse
    In Dickens and in Donne.

He thinks he'll make a Chair before
    He's thirty-eight or so;
His latest work is due out soon
    On Methuen Video.

Archaic bourgeois structures must
    Dictate a bourgeois text:
That methodology once grasped,
    It's hermeneutics next.

He's a brand-new desk computer
    For poems he takes to bits.
'The author's dead', you understand;
    In his place our Ernest sits.

READER

"We've colleagues so crazed about *relevance*, now,
That they'll set strip cartoons as a classroom text.
Like a page of Jane Austen, is that what they mean?
It's such eyewash" she adds. "I ask you, what next?"

There in her bookcase, the Cadell Walter Scott.
"One gets, don't you know, so frightfully weary
Of all this infernal jargon and piejaw
Of -ology, -ism and theory of theory;

It's so utilitarian, and it deprives
The young of their rights to the classics they need ..."
On the bureau below the 'Wordsworth' by Shuter
Lies her Blackwood's edition of *Adam Bede*.

SPORTS FIELD, SOUTH MANCHESTER

Hands numb, lungs rasping – about one tenth alive –
I whistle up. Touch-down? Knock-on? Scrum five?
Don't know. Don't care. The try line's lost in snow,
While the wind-chill factor chills like ten below.
My borrowed boots are pinching, and they hurt.
The sweat has turned to ice inside my shirt.

"Stamp your authority on the game; you're boss"
They said. But Lord, this is ridiculous;
It's *sleeting* now. Oh I'm an ace BF
For promising to come and effing ref.
What Paradise is like, though, I see clear:
A long, hot bath, a bar and lots of beer.

SLOTH

Sweet-talking, ever-present voice,
good friend and old familiar,
tyre round the midriff, treble-chinned,
long hopeful-travelling non-arriver –
though gross in size, you still retain
such silver-toned and subtle charm
that your tongue works like mandragora;

whose words (more sensitive-unerring than
the most ultrasonic microwave device)
will always home direct in on
that recess in our hearts
where deep complaisance lurks –
unswervingly, hypnotically;
wizard malingerer, loveable skrimshanker.

GERMAN LESSON: SUB-TEXT

She stands *behind* a chair *beside* the clock
Beneath the portrait *on* the mantelshelf.
It's Gertrud Muller, merchant Muller's wife;
"Herr Smith, now let me introduce myself".

How are you – very well – and did you take
The stopping train – oh yes, and then the bus,
Which left at half-past five (*halb sechs*, that is,
As Fraulein, with a halb-smile, says to us).

Herr Muller has a nose, two ears, dark hair,
A jacket and a tie, a brief-case, *so*,
But Fraulein, as you state this, *ironisch*,
There're other things we're bursting, like, to know:

Love-talk words, for instance – right pitch and right tone, too,
Oh let's doff grammar-clothes. Your eyes suggest it. Do.

CRITICAL REVIEW, OR DON'T FLY OFF THE HANDLE

From what he writes, you'd think the End was Nigh,
(I've known the feeling often, at Turf Moor:
The team quite *terrible*, the ref a fiend,
And three goals down, and Armageddon sure).

From what he writes, reviewing some poor sap,
You're put in mind of rape, or sacrilege;
Anathema and curse! How is it books
Provoke such high intensity of rage?

Forgo your verbal *Schadenfreude*, please,
Don't shoot the sap, he's done his level best;
Incongruous excess of phrase recalls
Don Quixote, Almaviva and the rest –
Those archetypes of all that's comic-sad ...

Recalls, as well, the critics Mozart had.

IN THE WINDOW OF A CITY CENTRE ANTIQUE SHOP

The spotlights halo, soft as bloom,
    Commode, cheval-glass, secretaire;
"What lovely things!" you say; and sigh;
    For stuff like that works out so dear.

So *we* can't murmur, back at home,
    To guests, with ease, with airiness,
"So nice to have such *nice* things round!"
    Those emblems of good taste, success.

Our dull and rented furnishings
    In job lots, cheap, the landlord bought.
Must nice things one day witness how
    Love's grown to need their mute support?

YVOIRE
for the Withdick-Pates

Midnight, now, and not a soul
on terrace, seat or lawn;
the empty promenade is paved
by geometries of shadow, all's still,
the atmosphere like vacuum –
except for where
a cowl of motionless and swarthy pines
steep-hems the harbour, close,
and the port's eye, restless, glitters.
How muscular and coal-glaze waves
in its rock-dark cockpit swell,
each bulge and buckle, seesaw tilt and hump,
by star-reflections ridden –
slippery, spilt mercury.
How exhaustlessly, with glob and plock,
the water, nervy, slaps
the rib and keel
of twenty tethered yachts,
white-hulled, compact as shells
and as perfect in their shapes,
in line, there, at the groyne.
How brittle, tense and taut
like highly-strung and
tight-reined colts they strain.

And what an eerie dance of sound
the halyards and the rigging make
on high spar and on creaking mast,
with tap-tap fret and horse's bridle clink.
Paths and grass are hushed, all's absence there,
yet how the white yachts bob and toss
as in a weird infectious chafe of desire,
charging the midnight dark
with electricity of expectation.

ON THE ABTHORPE ROAD

'Cut vines and osier
Plash hedge of enclosure'
– *Tusser Feby's Husbandrie*, quoted in Thomas Sternberg's
The Dialect and Folklore of Northamptonshire

Tonsured trim as suburb box,
This hawthorn hedge, *en brosse*,
Invests the lane with change –
With city stylishness.

No need of men to plash
The upright hedge-stems, now,
To peg them, chopped and bent,
Above cleared ditches' brow

To familiar thick-set frame.
This tonsure shows us how things go.
The plashing of hawthorn here
Was a human craft, but slow.

Quick and cheap, the powered shears,
So farmers, accounting, can subtract
Hedge-setting from man-hours.
Necessity's frame, in fact,

Confronts my weekender's eyes,
Who'd foist Arcadia where
Profit and loss oblige.
Most hedges began as Enclosure.

Across accountable land
A silo in sunlight glints neat.
'Silo' one's come to understand.
'Plash' will soon be obsolete.

GLOUCESTERSHIRE ALLIANCE, 1985

Reading the sports page through, I see
That Tewkesbury Rovers went two up
Last week, at Wick, through goals by Lea;
That Wilmcote won the John Wood Cup;

But Adlestrop – *they* crashed 4–1
At home to Chadlington, it seems,
Positioned here (some *cachet* gone)
Among the local soccer teams

Of Oxfordshire and Gloucestershire.
So evening *Stars* and *Mercuries*
Encompass matches everywhere
In small print mid-March summaries –

A bit like hawthorn hedged about
Rough pitches marked on rec and field
Year after year close-mapping out
Dense worlds of Trophy, Cup and Shield.

Near clinker lanes, allotment ends,
By pond and pylon, swing and slide,
Flower marginal and countless grounds
For fellowship, all England-wide,

Evoking countless memories
Now, as in twenty-, fifty-five,
Of shot, save, tackle, move and miss:
Quixotic, teeming, rich, alive.

Turf hushed tonight, in dark and dews,
Under perennial, damp-charged sky;
Where ghostly figures, stamping shoes,
Watch ghost-teams fight their needle tie.

THINKING OF MATTHEW ARNOLD ON THE M62
for Park and Jeannette Honan

"To see things as they really are", you wrote;
    But it was northern slum-schools you saw true,
        With Bradshaw's lines to con, not Greek, each day,
    Linking those factory towns you journeyed to.
        Amid such "grimness, bareness", then, what "stay" –
        From all you loved remote?
    Each night to lodgings you returned
        From days passed marking notes on algebra
        Or school-books ("dirty, ditto furniture");
    A poet into HMI transformed.

On one side, half-fed children, stunted growth,
    The working slums, girls in mills and mines;
        What could "ennoble" this, what "animate"?
    And then the middle class, your "Philistines",
        More passionate for railways than for "light" –
        And you estranged from both.
    What you saw truly, time and time again,
        Was something poetry could never feed,
        Nor urging dreams of Greece, and man's sore need
    For Homer, "simple, rapid, noble, plain".

You wrote your *Scholar Gypsy*, then, as well,
    Those timeless Berkshire fields a world away
        From schools in Blyth and York, reports to pore,
    Three hundred orals taken in one day,
        And pupil-teacher papers, by the score:
        The spiritual. The real.
    Your scholar sought pure self, intuitive,
        Neglectful of career, the world of men;
        In what dour digs did you conceive, and when,
    That symbol of free spirit, and that myth?

What of them now? Pure self, "ennoblement"?
    We've read so much; we're modern, knowing, wise.
        "His thin red line of verse, still holding out?"
    We joke of him, sat warm in Faculties,

Distrusting dreams, ironical about
  His "touchstones" ... tolerant.
For fifty-one per cent can now afford
  Their central heat, and ninety have TV;
  O brave new liberal democracy,
Where one in five now holidays abroad!

How out of date he feels! What dreams he had!
  I speed across the Pennines. I, too, teach.
    Lamplight and headlight shape things frosty-clear.
We're turning Shakespeare into common speech,
    And Greek's been lost, the tongue he held so dear;
      It's how things go. Too bad.
Great boards of blue and white unlyrically
    Highlight Leeds and Pontefract; snowflakes fall;
    Unfestal bulbs prink out a Bingo Hall;
On a blankness of Clearway, trucks thwack by.

MARKET STREET

In a wash of autumn crowds, we stop to kiss goodbye;
    You've only just got time to buy some things for tea.
You're sorry, but there, you've a family to cook for;
        I'm so lucky, you add. I'm free.

We stop to kiss goodbye. Then I am free to go,
    With prospects wide as seas, yes, choice on every hand;
The town my oyster, each evening hour my own,
        And life my kingdom to command.

Dear, do you covet this, my range of liberty,
    Weighed down by shopping, in the store's slow queue?
If you could only sense how blank its compass seems
        As I walk up Market Street, away from you.

IN NOVEMBER

In November, when the elm has shed
Its yellowed leaves across the asphalt's grey,
And suburb gusts and traffic slipstreams sweep
Them under our parked cars,
Against the whitewashed stones,
In at the double-doors,
New vistas open up, of winter muddy skies;
In summer vision's circumscribed by green,
But now we see the single magpie come,
Flash of satin blue upon his side,
To trespass in the forecourt here.
Most days he comes, to make me wonder why
He sticks to these few outskirts acres, so;
Surmise he knows
He can scavenge in old safety here, heeds
By instinct sheer necessity. Which same force,
Perhaps, determines more than his winged life;
May drive, unconsciously,
Our morning faces out to shops
For bread each day; and tempt small cars with Ls
At snail's pace three-point turns and starts and stops
Year-round in neighbouring streets; and infiltrate
Buff envelopes demanding rates
Inside each house in spring; and make
The tinny bells of brick St Chad's
Chime Sunday services; and drain
Dull whiteness from the sky just now,
Hardening street-lamp ingots of fluorescent light
Against the gloom; and compel each twenty-two
Half-hourly past our stop,
From Urmston to Levenshulme, and back.

BLOOM

A stone's throw off from Brian's Grill, and where
I'd booked the joke, 'the backroom with a view'
(Wet yards, asbestos roofs, bike-wheel and weeds,
Some panes of cloud, and much like Stockport, too)
Lay Eccles Street and Bloom's; which was, I saw,
Good Georgian, derelict; for which, I know,
Developers have blueprints planned, like home,
For high-rise slabs; and like home, good will go.

From dives round Abbey Street pulsed sounds of rock,
Since Dublin's internationalist these days;
I traced Bloom's path, from pilgrim interest,
That Everyman whose thoughts still emblemize
A human scale – provincial, decent, deep –
Our noise-nagged, cash-crazed polities hold cheap.

IN MEMORY OF PATRICK KAVANAGH

By lower Baggot Street, I found your lock:
Near Maxol Car Wash and where office towered
On each hand high, your poem and your bench –
The Dublin air with traffic thick and soured.

It should have been so otherwise, not flawed;
The oil-brown water scummed; the dripping gate;
A plastic bag; grey spars of two-by-one.
That haunted place should be inviolate.

Such stony ground a let-down, I recalled
The sunset conjuring a mist of light
From mica-specks within the granite grain
Along Dun Laoghaire harbour's huge sea-wall,
As if brute rock bore life. The way the song
You conjured out of stoniness lives on.

HOME THOUGHTS FROM THE KIMBERLEYS, WA

Where corellas, disturbed,
set up their hoarse shriek
above paperbarks lining
this unearthly-still creek,

an escarpment cliff-face
millions of years old
burns in the sun-glare
dark-tawny, pale gold –

to remind me, bizarrely,
of the rust-coloured stone
of Northamptonshire farms
I know well from home.

Unlikeness and likeness:
how we crave to relate
to the utter remoteness
of time beyond date –

like readings my mind's eye
brings vainly to bear
on horizons in a heat-pall
harsh bird-screams tear.

Off dirt-tracks, odd homesteads
bear names, too, that tell
what haunted first settlers:
Glencoe, Lissadell.

SYDNEY BRICK

The city's rich with one Lancastrian thing –
And that's red-brick. The good-bad-poem sort:
Some looks like raw rump steak, some's lobsterish;
Some's rosé pale; some shines like ruby port.

Some's apoplectic mauve and cheek by jowl
With glazed red-brick with Kranski sausage hues;
A red mosaic sprawl across the hills
From Ryde to Marrickville to La Perouse;

Maroon or fiery or plain ruddy brown,
Each one's red-brick beams out its different glow
In Bronte, Abbotsford and Wollstonecraft,
From school, shop, duplex, block and bungalow;

With constant startle, eyesight almost aches,
As Sydney brick in Sydney sunshine bakes.

A JAR WITH GLEN FITZGERALD: EXPOSTULATION AND REPLY

The Brits are Poms, OK. But when I press,
The Scots, I find, and Welshmen, are alright.
Press further then. Northumbrian? Or Scouse?
Or Brummie, Geordie, Dorset, Isle of Wight?
Press Catholic Scots, press Presbyterian;
Press Lancs v Yorks, what Wearside thinks of Tyne;
What Cornishmen of Devon men will say –
We're Poms are we? Well, come on, Glen, *define!*
To blazes Men of Kent and Wiganers?
The devil take all Lincoln folk and Tykes?
To hell with, what, soft Pommie Bristol burr?
The cockney of Sam Weller or Bill Sikes?
O richer far than poverty of Pom,
Can't each one differ, as and where they're from?

Fitzgerald replies
What Pom means, mate, is things like Bodyline;
It's the hypocrisy that makes us sick;
The steel below the well-bred velvet voice;
The will to win by any lousy trick.

You coined the phrase Fair Play, the Game's the Thing,
The Amateur, Good Sport – fair dos, that's fine
(It's Taking Part and Not the Winning Counts ...)
Then Poms invented bloody Bodyline.

PRAYER

St Christopher, protect us, please,
   From man with his Sony Walkman set,
Afraid of silence as of speech –
   Locked in his headphones' *oubliette*;

O comfort those compelled to hear
   His ceaseless double concerto tape
For bluebottle and squeaky chalk
   In train or bus, and no escape;

Look kindly on the traveller
   Condemned to eavesdrop group or band
Whose constant unoiled-wheel-cum-whizz
   Is more than flesh and blood can stand.

PICASSO, LATE DRAWINGS, AT GENEVA

Pornographie de vieillard!
Dieu te punira!

In the remarks' book at the Picasso show
The bold but childlike script condemns,
Condemns. Punish the old pornographer!
   Sees breast, hair, buttocks, lip and limbs,

Refracted by loving, derided sense;
Ageless the lady: so alive and assured!
To the dance of desire, like a lap-dog,
   Art's irrespressibly lured:

Where, as the dancer, it shines. And those prim words
Of jealous, self-righteous, primitive hate
Scald in the air-conditioning.
   Who said that we'd progressed, of late?

PRODIGAL

It's hard, when you think of it, not to feel
Considerable sympathy lurk
For the parable prodigal's brother –
The one who got on with his work,

Husbanding cattle, tilling the fields,
And dependably helping his dad,
While his sibling waltzed off with the money,
Then careered downhill to the bad.

For all that you see the father's point
About the son lost and then found,
There's a case to make for the one who stayed put,
Industrious, loyal and sound.

No wonder he took his father to task –
What happened was more than enough:
The spendthrift returned; the fatted calf hoopla;
The music and dancing and stuff.

Salvation and Grace to all sinners
Is of course what the moral entails;
But why should thanksgiving so wholly involve
The brother who went off the rails?

Aren't the values of journeyman duty
Meet, too, to make merry, be glad,
As much as contrition and heartfelt remorse
From a penitent Jack the Lad?

To forgiving's disproportionate joy
One defers (*felix culpa*) – yet, Lord,
Must we accept that devoted long service
Should suffice as its own damned reward?

OH

Oh, to get poems
   back on the page –
not ode as performance
   or stanza on stage,
but print in a book
   with words we may hear
in solitude speak
   to the inner ear,
and which, when we choose,
   we may re-read
in the freedom of quiet –
   for inner need.

LETTERS

"Dear Johns", they are called –
   in effect, just as if
it is always the lady
   who ups and goes off;

yet the phrase, with its hint
   of Woman as Eve,
("walked out on her fellow,
   now would you believe?"),

takes little account
   of that final "Dear Ann"
sent off by old Adam
   when *he* cut and ran.

CONTEXT, PROFILE, IMAGE, IMPACT, MISSION

Viewed in the Context of Profile and Image
  most managements now require,
we're not, as a big department goes, the sort
  "to set the Thames on fire";

a river which (think of it) burst into flame
  for sure would have Impact;
as Mission, though, what would the point be,
  viewed in a Context of fact?

BLURB

These poems are "sassy", says the blurb,
  To lead you to surmise
That knowingness spells knowledge now;
  Street wisdom equals wise.

ST OLAF'S, WASDALE HEAD

St Olaf's church at the dalehead stands
In peace beyond the gloomy Screes;
Where the vicar from 'forty to 'forty-one
Was the Reverend George O'Cheese.

THOMAS BEWICK

Your graver's tempered steel
From dead grain yields its line;
Fur-soft, smoke-lithe or exact
As a brim's stir in your Tyne.

You "stuck to nature closely",
Despite laborious means,
Cutting your peacock's fan –
Your drunk, who sees two moons –

Your unconventional,
Unclassical thrush and lark;
"Beautiful aireal wanderers",
Immediate and life-like.

And so – a temperate,
God-fearing, dyed-in-the-wool,
Individualistic,
Northumbrian provincial –

You revived the lost skills
Of the craftsman-engraver;
Both deviser-designer
And populariser.

*

Can revolutionary art
Have been ever so modest
As yours, Thomas Bewick?
Who in "kitchen work" traced

On blocks inches square
"Nature up to nature's God",
Creating an Empire from
One parish neighbourhood,

To establish the mystery
Of boxwood engraving –
That fine-as-leaf-vein craft,
Demotic, moral, loving.

WILLIAM PAYNE

In Plymouth City Gallery,
  One Christmas Eve, all rain,
I saw a retrospective
  Of painter "Payne's Grey" Payne,
Whose name will mean forever
  That earthy, darkish hue
He mixed from yellow ochre,
  Lake and Prussian blue.

More dense than Indian ink,
  Those Payne's grey washes made
The middle distance deeper,
  With shade that looked like shade,
In picturesque topography
  And local landscape view,
Like Mutton Cove or Pengersick,
  Or Stonehouse Hill or Looe.

From the swan baptised as Bewick's,
  Via Banks's Banksia rose
To Canon Greenwell's Glory,
  Payne stands foursquare with those
Whose names fused with the language
  And still survive today:
A waterfowl; a flower;
  A dry-fly – and a grey.

Eponymously genial,
  They were creators who
Described the nondescript,
  If small-scale, no less new;
Extending our awareness,
  Enriching the mundane –
Like a wet-through day enhanced
  Through meeting William Payne.

GOOD HUSBANDRY

Good husbandry: a phrase to hint at life
Whose ends cohere, in harmony with means;
Far-sighted; sane; frugal as coppicing,
One with the earth as each new season greens.

To what avail, such prescient foresight, when
Some highday binge, unbargained for, transpires –
Release from order, break-out from routine?
Drink deep for here and now; light roaring fires.

You can't but see how anarchy appeals,
Uplifted as you must be as you gaze,
For all its waste, its short-term, spendthrift spell:
A useless, consuming, marvellous blaze.

D.I.Y.

Out the gnarled bricks of the old fireplace come:
Down-to-basics world. Black-and-Decker-dom.
Mortar-clogged my nails, grime and soot in hair,
And rubble-dust's hoar-frost on shelf and chair,
I drill, then tap, then lever, coax – and *thump!*
The buggers crash in dirt-plumes, lump on lump.

And next by stages built up, bit by bit,
Clean lengths of timber in the gape's gap fit.
A joist's cemented in to hold the weight;
An upright braced; a chamfer chiselled straight;
The saw is urged through softwood 2 x 2;
Then mouldings mitred, millimetre true.

Framework to finish, the firm structure grows;
From mind and muscle matched, enjoyment flows.
At length there's plastering, to plumb-line cord,
Undercoat and topcoat, smooth as a board –
Sponged flush, dried out, and sanded well when set,
Then painted thrice ... This world's compact. Complete.

Compared to such plain work, poems seem unreal.
That architrave, that surface, now: just *feel!*
Yet soon to worlds less sure, the mind returns;
Lamplight on papers in a far room burns.
So dusty, tingling, tired – achievement-dry –
My hand takes up the pen. But doubtfully.

LANE

Upgrading once decided on,
the County Council set about
this Heart of England grass-verged lane
which goes from Litchborough to Duncote,
cementing kerbstones at each edge.
Now in the April evening light,
instead of ditch and hawthorn hedge,
your eye is held by a die-straight white
perspective of official kerb;

more country gone for more suburb.

ON THE ROAD

Low sun from Bradden way reflects
a paleness like hoar-frost
off moisture left on winter wheat
by vanished early mist;

where all is still, save kneading swarms
of mote-sized morning midges,
hovering just above the mud
of tyre-stamped road-side ridges;

whose hour-long insect lives must have
their due purpose, I daresay,
in a general scheme of things,
and part or bit-part to play –

yet perturb the outward stillness
and answering inner peace,
and whether we like it or no
cannot and will not cease.

ENVOI

Hadyn/Hofstetter (?) String Quartet Op 3 No 5

for Paddy and Nina Stephenson

We may never know for sure
Who wrote that haunting serenade;
But as Haydn has so much more,
Let Hofstetter not be denied –
So he may shine, a minor star,
In excellence a singleton,
Like Eichner, Litolf and such men
Whom genius touched, it seems, by chance,
Just once.

Note on 'John Glover', p. 6.

John Glover was a commercially successful, good if derivative,
painter in the 18th century picturesque arcadian tradition in
England. He had houses in London and, for a spell, in Patterdale
in the Lakes. In 1831, at the age of 63, he emigrated to Tasmania
(Van Diemans Land) to join his farmer-sons. He settled on an
estate near Launceston, calling it Patterdale, near the Tasmanian
Esk and under Ben Lomond. Here, inspiritingly, he became the
first substantial painter-interpreter of the Australian landscape.
Although his many later works still owe something to European
(Claudian), precedent, it is surprising how originally 'Australian'
they look. Robert Woof, secretary of the Wordsworth Trust at
Dove Cottage, has helped to show how Glover played a part in
opening up the Lakes as a subject for landscape painters. (*The
Lake District Discovered*, exhibition catalogue, The Trustees of
Dove Cottage, 1983)

Note on 'Haydn/Hofstetter ...', p. 64.
I am grateful to the late Kingsley Amis for pointing out that the
piece is a serenade (not a minuet, as I wrongly wrote at first),
and suggesting a half-rhyme to go with the right word.